I Can Pray!

WRITTEN BY JENNIFER HOLDER AND DIANE STORTZ

ILLUSTRATED BY C. A. NOBENS

© 2001, 2005 Standard Publishing, Cincinnati, Ohio. A division of Standex International Corporation. All rights reserved. Printed in the United States of America. Cover design: Robert Glover. Scripture quotations are taken from the Holy Bible, *New Living Translation,* copyright © 1996. Used by permission of Tyndale House Publishers, Inc., Wheaton, Illinois 60189. All rights reserved.

ISBN 0-7847-1694-3

11 10 09 08 07 06   9 8 7 6 5

Standard®
PUBLISHING
Bringing The Word to Life

Cincinnati, Ohio

I can pray!

Praying is talking and listening to God.

I have lots of things to say to God
in my prayers.

When I pray, I praise God.
God is awesome and powerful.
God does wonderful things
every day.

When I pray, I confess

the things I have done wrong.

When I ran through

Mrs. Nelson's flower beds,

I prayed to God.

I told him I had done something wrong.

When I pray, I thank God for his blessings.
I tell him I am grateful
for my family, friends, and church.

When I pray, I ask God for his help.

I ask him to help other people.

When my friend's dad was sick,

I asked God to help him get better,

and he did!

Give all your worries and cares to God.

—1 Peter 5:7

God wants me to talk to him,

but he also wants to talk to me.

I listen to God when I read the Bible.

The Bible is God's Word.

God helps me know what is right.

God is always near me,

listening to my prayers.

There are lots of different ways to pray.

Sometimes I kneel at my window.

I can write or draw a prayer.

Whether my prayer is loud or quiet,

God will hear it.

Even though I can't see God's face,

I know he is listening.

No matter where I am or how I do it,
I can pray . . .

and God will always, always listen.

Keep on praying.

—1 Thessalonians 5:17